BERLIN HANOVER EXPRESS

T0353302

Ian Kennedy Martin

BERLIN HANOVER EXPRESS

OBERON BOOKS
LONDON

First published in 2009 by Oberon Books Ltd
521 Caledonian Road, London N7 9RH
Tel: 020 7607 3637 / Fax: 020 7607 3629
e-mail: info@oberonbooks.com
www.oberonbooks.com

A catalogue record for this book is available from the British
Library.

ISBN: 978-1-84002-901-7

Cover design by Kamil Krawczyk

Introduction

I spent four years in Ireland in the late fifties. There I first heard that Prime Minister de Valera had signed the condolence book at the German Legation on the death of Hitler. Neutral Ireland had a German legation in Dublin throughout the war, and Ireland had a legation in Berlin. I may have been a little naïve about some Germans I met in Dublin. I later learned Ireland had been one of the key staging posts on Germany's collapse for getting various Nazis out of their country and on to resettle in other parts of the world. Invited to the flat of one guy, I saw on his mantlepiece a card written in German. I asked for a translation, he obliged – 'I wonder what made God choose the Jews'. The Catholic Church and certain government immigration people had conspired together bringing in the Nazis because like many in the German High Command they shared Roman Catholicism. And also because the Irish Catholic Church had always been casually anti-Semitic.

I could not understand Ireland's neutrality. By 1942 it was known that the Holocaust was up and running. So why were Ireland and other neutral countries turning a resolute blind eye to this genocide? Of course Germany was in many ways more a friend to Ireland than Britain whose repulsive wrecking behaviour over Eirenn had gone on for two hundred years. Also the Brits had only been foiled at one point from executing de Valera because he was an American. At any event I came to a conclusion about the generality of the idea of a country's neutrality in a time of war – if you are neutral you are on the side of an enemy. Any neutral country that stands between two warring factions, one with right on its side, the other not, is tacitly supporting the aggressor. This is the theme examined in the play *Berlin Hanover Express* in its setting of the Irish Legation in Berlin in 1942.

Ian Kennedy Martin

Characters

O'KANE

MALLIN

CHRISTE

KOLLVITZ

Berlin Hanover Express was first performed at Hampstead Theatre, London on 5 March 2009 with the following cast:

MALLIN   Sean Campion
CHRISTE   Isla Carter
O'KANE   Owen McDonnell
KOLLVITZ   Peter Morteon

Director   Michael Rudman
Designer   Paul Farnsworth
Lighting Designer   David Howe
Sound Designer   Colin Pink

Act One

The main office in the Irish legation, Berlin, late 1942.

The war is at its height, the Berlin working day interrupted by air raids and false alarms. The two Irish legation officials MALLIN and O'KANE exist in this capital to 'promote trade' (not much of that), deal with passports and visas, and look after the thousand plus Irish ex-pats and businessmen living in the Reich.

The legation occupies half of a small building in Konstanzer Strasse.

The main office is two desks, filing cabinets, and a table where meals are snatched. Over the larger of the desks, MALLIN's, displayed on the wall, the crossed flags of the Irish tricolour and the German Swastika in black against red. On the other wall a large map of Germany.

The third member of staff is FRAULEIN CHRISTE MOLLER. She cooks for the two and their visitors. Off stage a dining room when the limited variety of food becomes available, MALLIN and O'KANE entertain parties of diplomats, businessmen, or other Irishmen.

Curtain up on MALLIN and O'KANE at their desks, piled with papers.

Centre stage a tea chest. The stencilled 'Magawatee Ceylon Tea' has been crossed through and 'Valise diplomatique Republique d'Irelande, Berlin' hand written in heavy black capitals.

O'KANE gets up from desk with a sheaf of papers, moves to tea chest and drops them in, goes back to his desk, studies MALLIN reading memos, notes, telexes from one large pile, putting them into another.

O'KANE is a Dublin man, MALLIN from Kildare.

O'KANE: A joke.

MALLIN looks, irritated.

MALLIN: What?

O'KANE: A joke.

MALLIN: (*Groans.*) Christ.

O'KANE: It's short. An Englishman, an Irishman and a Scotsman…

MALLIN: (*Interrupts.*) I've heard it.

O'KANE: You haven't heard it.

MALLIN: Anyone I haven't heard I don't wish to hear.

O'KANE: Why not?

MALLIN: Why?

O'KANE: God almighty it's just fecking pleasantries, a little humour brought into our sodding drab lives.

MALLIN: When was the last time you heard an Irish joke that was humorous?

O'KANE: I'm going to tell you one.

MALLIN: You're not. I don't want my brain filled with shite by your mindless prattle.

O'KANE: It's insults now?

MALLIN: Yes.

Pause. Then O'KANE puts on a 'bog Irish' accent.

O'KANE: You're a feckin' intemperate bowsy with a sense of humour of a mutton knuckle. You're a hoyden scurravogue with brains of a bog trotter and the manners of a dullamoo.

MALLIN: Enough!

MALLIN continues reading, finishes a pile, gets up, heads to the chest, drops papers in.

O'KANE: I'm not to talk at all at all? A Bejesus business, no mind meetings, no debatings, two of the damned in a pit of silence.

MALLIN: I've noted with dismay the recent arrival into your language of certain, what is it, music hall slang? Until a while ago you spoke properly.

O'KANE: English? I'm not feckin English. God no.

MALLIN: Whether you're speaking English or gutter Irish do neither.

O'KANE glares, waits. Then –

O'KANE: There were an old couple, both parted the four score, come into this style of a workman's caff, and they order...

MALLIN: We have this report to make in the next few days. A report that says we have read and assessed every piece of correspondence, every named contact, every journey Fahy made in his three years here in Berlin. Hundreds of papers and memos. I can't work if you're sitting there gobbing crap.

O'KANE: I'm readin'...studyin' away.

MALLIN: And you'd better be more careful trawling your nightlife after the curfew.

O'KANE: Why? I have been stopped. I just showed them my diplomat laisser-passer.

MALLIN: They may shoot you before they check your pass.

O'KANE: Don't look so cheerful saying that. And by the way, my last Will and Testamentary is held by the landlord of Neary's, a great man for the finest watering hole.

MALLIN: How in God's name you ever got into the diplomatic service. There, I've said it. I've been thinking a year without saying it. Now it's said. The next time, written in words, a long memo back to Dublin.

O'KANE: Who says you have to listen to me? I'm by way of talking to meself, keeping me own company, telling stories, reminiscences, jokes. There's no one else see? You're about as forthcoming as a tongueless man and about as lyrical. I don't know who grounded you in such humourlessness. You Protestants take full blame.

MALLIN: Enough of that!

O'KANE: One joke and I'll be silent.

MALLIN: Christ…!

O'KANE: So the old man and the woman they come into this style of a caff, and they order one sausage – one egg on one plate and one piece of toast and two knives and two forks…

MALLIN: I'm your senior officer O'Kane and I'm ordering you to work. Fahy, his friends the Norwegians, any conduits to the Brits.

O'KANE: You knew the man for near three years. You know Fahy wasn't a spy.

MALLIN: We do what we're ordered. We read these papers. For our German hosts, for our Dublin bosses who have given us the task and our employment.

O'KANE: But you said yourself in your opinion Fahy was no spy.

MALLIN ignores.

You can hurt a man.

MALLIN: What?!

O'KANE: You think I shouldn't be in the Foreign Service. You doubt my intellect, talent.

MALLIN: Yes! Yes I do!

O'KANE: You ask how I got into the Foreign Service.

MALLIN: I don't want to hear it.

O'KANE: I was astride the motorbike on the way to Killeen somewhere near Oughterard. A beautiful day, clear skies with the rain skeetin sideways as if to water the sea barnacles on church roofs. At a roundabout called comically 'World's End' both wheels fell off the veyhicle and I ended up well imprinted on the mass of a brick wall. I came to and standing there was the Angel Gabriel, a little worse for wear, you could smell drink taken. He pronounced, 'Go forth Fergal and take the exams of the Irish Foreign Service.' And so I did and passed. What a shitehawk that Gabriel. He was surely punishing me for sins like tupping me landlady at her regular high velocity as would land her clear off the mattress and out of the bed.

MALLIN: Are you going to work or not?

O'KANE: I'm doing it. I been reading. I've done maybe a hundred pages. And I'm writing. Poor Fahy and his non spying achievements. You've said he was a boring little man. Why do we have to make the finds against the lad? They've got a bunch of gobeens back at Dublin foreign ministry glad for any work.

MALLIN: The gobeens as you call them do not know Berlin from Bremen, Dusseldorf from Breslau.

O'KANE: Nor will we if the Brits go on bombing us personally. Let me finish me one joke. So this old couple go into this style of a caff, order the one egg, the one sausage, the one slice of toast, and they sit and the husband cuts the egg in a neat half, the sausage likewise, and the toast likewise and he commences to eat the halves as the old woman watches.

MALLIN gets up, goes to filing cabinet.

Hear me in there? (*Loud voice.*) So there is in this style of a caff seated, a generous farmer, possibly from Kilkenny or such and he's seeing these old folks, and he goes over to them and he offers, putting it like, 'Friends, I was once as poor as a cathedral mouse with no farthings to my pocket and no coat on me back. I see you order only one egg, one sausage and one toast and I would like to offer you, paying meself for it, a second plate of the same commoluments so as you might be more fulsomely fed. I see you share everything to such precision as to cut the egg and then the sausage and the pan slice in halves, but perhaps I'm surprised that the husband o' yourselves is the first to eat the halves. Is there an explanation for this?' The old man continued to eat away while his wife offered explanation,

MALLIN slams filing cabinet shut.

'Well,' she says quiet and patently saintlike, 'I'm waiting for the teeth…' I'M WAITING FOR THE TEETH…!!

O'KANE laughs wildly at his own joke. MALLIN ignores.

MALLIN: You finished?

O'KANE: A good one well told, yes?

MALLIN: I'm looking for the one clear example of your incompetence or stupidity and I will report you to Dublin to have you recalled. By Christ, I mean it.

O'KANE: But you could be slightly buggered there, right? Buggered. Admit it. You're senior officer, but me dad is the friend of de Valera. Or is that a challenge?

MALLIN: One clear example.

O'KANE: One should be easy. By the way did you see the telegraph yesterday from our bosses? The word 'Emergency' is used three times.

MALLIN: So?

O'KANE: Explain.

MALLIN: What needs explanation?

O'KANE: The word 'Emergency'. What's your definition?

MALLIN: Ninety per-cent of everything that utters from your gob daily is a waste of time.

O'KANE: Open the door and peek. There's a world war out there. Nations slaughtering each other. Why do our government and its departments refer to this as an 'Emergency'? That's it, isn't it? Quote… (*He reads from teleprint.*)…'during the emergency' and here 'because of the Emergency.' An emergency suggests a sort of temporary crisis, a kind of twenty-four hour job. How come our government refers to an ever expanding huge war as an 'emergency'?

MALLIN: How would you refer to it?

O'KANE: A total worldwide fucking catastrophe.

MALLIN: Maybe you should put that in a note and send it to your family's great pal, de Valera.

O'KANE: I'll think about it. So you're only looking for one clear example of so called incompetence?

MALLIN: Yes.

O'KANE: After I was nearly bombed flat in Beilefeld the other week, and being as I'm fond of the way all me bits fit I might decide to help you. It's a thought.

MALLIN: How can you talk rubbish all the time?

O'KANE: Education. A rare Catholic boy degreed up in Trinity College learning Classics and Humanities, and you, a Proddy, a graduate of Dublin's National, where the sons of soil learn to plant praties, cut bog, serve mass and never question their Pope in Rome castle. Vision and culture versus abject medieval obedience.

MALLIN: You say you're denying your Roman Catholicism?

O'KANE: Except when the bombs are dropping on me head.

MALLIN: And you went to Trinity, a brothel for drunks and pederasts, without the excommunication of your Church?

O'KANE: I got the dispensation. De Valera knew my father. My father knows Dev. A nice man, odd in appearance, but once he'd taken his boots off, a hard drinking night till dawn lad, with of course intervals of haughmagandie with any passing lady.

MALLIN: So Trinity is where you learned cheapness and obscenity.

O'KANE: Little else. A Renaissance man.

MALLIN: I want to say something serious to you and I want you to listen.

O'KANE: Oh...

MALLIN: I have reason to have worries about you and our cook. Don't deny it. I saw your hand stray the other night as she was serving us.

O'KANE: She had her bottom pointing towards me, a crumb on it that needed a bit of a brush.

MALLIN: If you touch Fraulein Moller, I'll write to Dublin and inform the Berlin politzie.

O'KANE: I'm a Trinity man. You must be aware of rumours, Oscar Wilde, etcetera. So Fraulein Christe, is it perhaps the strong powerful joxer like yourself may be contemplating a move there? She is a capital lass.

MALLIN: I'm going to start making a note of some of these things you're saying.

O'KANE: I thought your time was fully occupied, you know, Fahy. Now if he was a spy I'm really the one who wants to nail him, string him up, hang him maybe in the bus station, Finglas.

MALLIN: You'd like to see a colleague hanged?

O'KANE: Being Anglo-Irish a small detail may have escaped you. Winston Churchill was Home Secretary for the Brits when he invented the Black and Tans and sent them butchering. Would you spy for a man like that, for a country like that? Is your loyalty somewhere in doubt, Derry Mallin?

MALLIN: I work for my country. You yap.

CHRISTE enters with tray of afternoon tea and sandwiches.

O'KANE: Miss Moller, did you know that Mr Mallin here is a Cromwellian? D'you know of Oliver Cromwell?

CHRISTE: I don't understand.

MALLIN: Don't listen to him.

O'KANE: He was an anti-Christ who brought boat loads of British murderers to Ireland to destroy us utterly. Still thousands of them around today thinking they're superior and worshipping the King of England as the head of their Church. (*To MALLIN.*) Right? I'm surprised Fahy wasn't one of your Protestants.

MALLIN: Fraulein Moller, Mr O'Kane is more half wrong than half right. I'm not a Catholic like this man. I did not go to a Catholic school. Daily I thank my god for that. I did go to a Catholic university, on a scholarship. My parents not having the money of Mr O'Kane's people. I got into the Foreign Service through work and initiative, not family pull. I resent being called a Cromwellian. My kin stood shoulder to shoulder with our fellow countrymen in all the battles for Ireland's independence.

O'KANE: And now he's shoulder to shoulder with your German leaders.

MALLIN: That's right. Mr O'Kane seems afraid to answer one question. Is Germany Ireland's friend and England her enemy? See what he answers.

O'KANE: I'm wit' youse. Because Fraulein Moller is a German and a wonderful cook and personality.

MALLIN: (*To CHRISTE.*) Mr O'Kane, did he tell you? Next Wednesday, the dinner.

CHRISTE: He didn't say how many.

MALLIN: They'll be six of us, just two courses will be enough. A junior consul representative of the Vichy French, a businessman from Switzerland. Von Kassler from External Affairs, and some Bavarian who has a financial interest in Dublin hotels. You give me your food order I'll phone diplomatic supplies.

CHRISTE: I can give you orders for the dinners. But I think there are even more shortages this month.

O'KANE: Mr Mallin will bend a few arms, maybe break a few.

She goes.

Thanks for the tea. (*To MALLIN.*) Question. (*Indicates tea chest.*) D'you think the carriers will reckon it's too large the yoke to be called the diplomatic bag? We've never sent something this big.

MALLIN: Anything we choose to call the diplomatic bag, from a parcel to a wardrobe, is the diplomatic bag.

O'KANE: In yours and Fahy's time here did you ever get a clue that our Berlin hosts ever opened our bag and had a peek?

MALLIN: The Foreign Service is honourable, and their powers exceed those of any security organisation. Why?

O'KANE: I've a fancy to send a Black Forest ham to me auld mother.

MALLIN: Even Herr Kollvitz couldn't find you a Black Forest ham.

There's the sound of an air raid siren.

Get moving.

O'KANE: I'm tired of that smelly shelter. Right?

MALLIN: Take the day book. I'll take the report logs.

O'KANE: Bollocks! The RAF only bomb Berlin when they think it's Munich.

As MALLIN exits with report logs.

Another good one. An Englishman and Irishman and a Scotsman go into a Chinese laundry with the twenty shillings between them…

To black.

Then –

CHRISTE clears away a meal she's served. She's alone with O'KANE.

The radio is on, a Goebbel's ranting speech.

O'KANE: I'm getting used to this main meal in the afternoon.

She says nothing.

A wonderful sunset for a beautiful day, bombs apart.

CHRISTE: Yes.

O'KANE: Yes?

CHRISTE: Yes.

O'KANE: You have a true monosyllabic way about you Christe. A yes and no approach to the world, no nonsense, no greys, white, and black. When you talk to your friends what do you say? I've rarely heard you utter two sentences.

CHRISTE: What should I talk about?

O'KANE: (*Shrugs.*) A beautiful day, like this.

CHRISTE: When I was young I was taken to the Zoological Garden by my parents. There was an old man there, an Italian, who sold ice creams from a push cart. He would ask me the names of certain flowers in the displays. If I could answer he would give me a free ice cream. Sometimes it was difficult. If there was warm winter the daffodils would come out so early when the buds should not be there at all. Then we would have a picnic beside the Spree. Thick bread and chicken and sometimes wine from Alsace. I was allowed a little taste. My father had an accordion and would play it right in the middle of the park and people would gather around and my mother and I would sing. There was a bierkeller near our house where my father would smoke his pipe and play chess, and I could sit there with a glass of lemonade and clap him when he won the games. He always won.

She goes silent. O'KANE is studying her.

O'KANE: Can I say something?

CHRISTE: Yes?

O'KANE: You're telling me a load of nonsense. That's fairy tale stuff isn't it? Picnics and daffodils and loving family. I seriously doubt it happens in real life. Tell me again about you and your family.

CHRISTE a hesitation, then –

CHRISTE: My father was always a distant man. He had a mistress, a girl from Vienna. She was sixteen. My mother knew about her. She did nothing except cry. She was so weak. I was the child who confronted him. All that happened was he became angry and spent less time at home. We lived a charade. He spent less money on us and his promise to me to go further with my English studies was broken. He would turn up and expect my mother to accompany him to certain social gatherings at his place of work, his bank. And he would criticise her for poor clothes even though he knew clothes money was now going to his mistress. He had some guilt so when he came home he was often drunk. That's how he dealt with the problem of having a family and no longer wanting them. He was drunk when he crashed the car and killed himself and my mother.

Long pause.

O'KANE: That I believe. The truth binds people together, the other tears them apart.

CHRISTE: I have wondered what is the truth about you, Herr O'Kane.

O'KANE: You wonder. A great man like myself in a shit hole like Berlin in this time of God. Well the truth is I have a medical problem. I'm nuts. This was spotted by the doctor advisers to our Foreign Service. 'The lad', they said, 'is apt to fail us in certain times, so you'd better stick him out with those Nazis in Germany. Those folks are so mad an Irish loony will pass unnoticed.' Here you have me.

CHRISTE: I think you are a good person.

O'KANE: I am that, and you can count on me, while we occupy the land of the living and not a bomb crater. You know, we should talk more.

CHRISTE: There's not a lot about me which makes good
conversation.

O'KANE: But you're all right now. You've fetched up in a
city being blitzed and buggered in the company of two
Irishmen. What better?

CHRISTE: You've been very good to me.

MALLIN enters.

MALLIN: Fraulein Moller. This last week, how many times has
Herr Kollvitz come here? After O'Kane and I leave for the
day.

CHRISTE: He's been…three times.

MALLIN: He brings food, you cook it, you eat together and he
leaves?

CHRISTE: Yes.

MALLIN: And we're grateful much of the food is for us. So
we're not saying we're not pleased, but we are concerned
a little about his visits. Obviously O'Kane and I have to
leave to get to our flats before curfew. Curfew doesn't seem
to apply to security men like Kollvitz. Yes?

CHRISTE: Yes.

O'KANE: How late does he stay?

CHRISTE: He leaves after I've cooked and he's eaten.
And… (*Hesitates.*)

MALLIN: And?

CHRISTE: He believes I am an excellent cook.

O'KANE: You are.

MALLIN: Does he ever discuss anything to do with our work
here?

CHRISTE: No.

MALLIN: Our legation may be only a few rooms but anyone entering here is stepping onto the soil of the Republic of Ireland and is subject to our law, not the laws of Germany.

O'KANE: I think Fraulein Christe knows this (*To CHRISTE.*) so if you get tired of him you don't have to open the door to him.

MALLIN: What O'Kane is trying to say is be careful with Herr Kollvitz. We gather he may be a more senior member of some investigation branch than he makes out. Such people can get the wrong ideas on occasion.

O'KANE: It may only be the lad fancies your cooking alone. You report to us if he gives you any kind of worries, right?

CHRISTE: Yes.

MALLIN: Fraulein Moller you report to me not to Mr O'Kane, right?

CHRISTE nods.

O'KANE is irritated by MALLIN's correction.

O'KANE: Christe.

CHRISTE: Yes?

O'KANE: I'd like to tell you how I got into the Diplomatic Service. I've had some questions about that.

MALLIN: Stop it, now.

O'KANE: I'm not addressing you. I'm speaking to Christe here. (*To CHRISTE.*) Would you not like to know how I got this posting in your admirable country?

CHRISTE: (*Uncertain.*) Yes.

MALLIN leaves table, goes over, turns up radio, resumes work at desk.

O'KANE helps CHRISTE clear up.

O'KANE: So it goes. My father the Fenian must have shot at least one Brit at the Post Office. He was an ace on the blunderbuss against Mayo Foxes and local Gombeen men. So he was known to de Valera and not unloved by our leader. So some night at the Dublin Opry, its 'Blue Blood' composed by a Rooshin or foreigner, Dev spots me dada and says, 'I hear your son is a champeen cyclist and won the Dublin Cork Open to all Comers prize on tandem with some priest on rear pedals.' The dada agrees. 'So he can con a priest into the hard work on back saddle. He must be some diplomat. We should give him a job.' So the dada phones the Foreign Service and says, 'Check with Dev but he says you're to give me son a job.' 'Right.' says the Foreign Service, 'But as a favour to me', the dada added, 'stick him into Berlin. It's known the Yankees and the Brits have the intention to bomb the place flat.' D'you like that story, Christe?

CHRISTE: I'm sure it's not true.

MALLIN: Mr O'Kane says little that's believable.

O'KANE: Sunshine and smile to people's lifes. That's what I believe.

CHRISTE collects tray, goes out.

Listen Derry Mallin, are we getting a little oversensitive, you know, your man, Kollvitz...

MALLIN: I want you to take care.

O'KANE: Why?

MALLIN: We don't know exactly what he represents, what's his role, his work.

O'KANE: I do. I asked him.

MALLIN: You did what?

O'KANE: I asked him, what do you do for your wages, Volker?

MALLIN: And?

O'KANE: He said he searched for Communists, Reds under the beds, plus other undesirables by which he means I guess, gypsies and Jews. But he kind of foamed at the mouth about the Commies. They were the real menace. They hadn't gone away. Course they were popular in Germany after the last Donnybrook.

MALLIN: Aware, is what we need to be. Always on our guard. Our position…

O'KANE: Care to read these telexes between Fahy and his Norwegians?

MALLIN: What?!

O'KANE: I found four, I think.

MALLIN: Why the Hell didn't you tell me?!

O'KANE: They're white as the driven snow. Come on! Fahy, whatever his weirdness, he did not spy for the Brits and then write memos and telexes giving his game away. You said he was a Cork man. They're a vicious gang down there but you won't find many fools.

O'KANE has handed some telexes to MALLIN. MALLIN scans them.

MALLIN: These messages could be coded.

O'KANE: (*Wry.*) Really? He writes coded messages to his Norwegians in Trelso who then pass them on to British Intelligence. 'British Intelligence' – now there's a laugh in itself. He writes 'Dear Sven. I'm away to Switzerland for briefest recreation. Please recommend the best skiing you think is about the place this time of year. Most grateful. Michael Fahy.' You think that can be decoded into Axis troop movements on the Rooshin Front?

MALLIN: If the subject of Fahy comes up with Herr Von Kollvitz I suggest you talk as if you're taking this seriously.

O'KANE: Nod me the wink. I'll take anything seriously. Even you.

Ring on the doorbell. CHRISTE enters with KOLLVITZ then exits.

KOLLVITZ is athletic but thin framed. In civilian clothes which suggest he's a bit of the affable dandy. But there's always threat just beneath the surface. As he enters O'KANE and MALLIN exchange looks. They are getting concerned about his visits.

KOLLVITZ: Did you have the chicken?

O'KANE: Brilliant. Its short life gifted with great meaning.

KOLLVITZ: It's becoming so hard to find fresh food now. Where does it go? In the confusion of war comes criminality. Many arrests, black marketeers, but every day they breed like flies.

O'KANE: (*Insincere.*) It's very good to see you Herr Kollvitz but perhaps as you're becoming a feature around here we should be on Christian name terms.

KOLLVITZ: Yes Fergal. And Mister Derry. But this time I'm not socialising, though I would prefer to. This time I have something official to discuss with you.

MALLIN: We have maybe half an hour before curfew.

KOLLVITZ: These curfews will soon be over. That's the good news.

O'KANE: Would you like some of the wine you kindly provided?

KOLLVITZ: Excellent. I believe there is an imminent arrival of the 1940 Bordeaux, a brilliant vintage.

O'KANE finds bottle and a glass in filing cabinet, pours, hands glass to KOLLVITZ.

O'KANE: I don't know how you get hold of this stuff Herr Kapitan.

KOLLVITZ: I've always thought the people of Ireland are our friends. So this is unfortunate that I have to say what has to be said. We are always delighted at your presence. But we have perhaps some problems. First, your Mister Michael Fahy now recalled to your country – our belief that he was working for our Reich's enemies.

O'KANE: Unproven.

KOLLVITZ: In your view.

O'KANE: Our view, yes.

KOLLVITZ: Now another problem. It has been brought to
our notice that your newspaper, the Irish Independent,
has printed a photograph. The Fitzwilliam Square Tennis
Competition in your capital.

MALLIN: We've heard.

KOLLVITZ: German officers seen in full military uniform
photographed at this tournament.

O'KANE: Exactly so what?

KOLLVITZ: Of course the officers will be disciplined – wearing
military uniforms in a neutral country. But clearly the
newspaper editor was at a mischief to publish this. This
is provocation. Officers make a foolish mistake and the
photograph is prominent in your national newspaper.

O'KANE: It's not my national newspaper. I'm an Irish Times
man.

KOLLVITZ: Your government should always be aware to look
out for propaganda which damages our relationship. You
are a neutral country, good. But as the time comes when
our nation has conquered Europe we will expect, no
demand, that countries like yours exercise discipline.

O'KANE: Quite.

MALLIN: Dublin, I understand, has apologised.

KOLLVITZ: Why would your editor publish this photograph
knowing it would be aggressive to us?

MALLIN: As honesty is on the table I guess there's currently
an amount of ill feeling back home since your Heinkels
dropped those bombs on North Strand near our capital.

KOLLVITZ: Everyone knows that was a mistake, a complete mistake, and you have knowledge of how those airmen were disciplined.

O'KANE: Still the bombs were dropped, maybe one near the editor of the Independent.

KOLLVITZ: Are you finding this funny?

O'KANE: No.

MALLIN: Don't listen to him. I apologise for this needless photo and yes I can see it as a provocation and I will communicate with our Home Office that they seriously caution the newspaper.

KOLLVITZ: Very good. So let me know what response you get. On the matter of Fahy…

MALLIN: We're on your case believe me. (*Points to piles of papers on desk and in tea chest.*) We're sifting through every paper and form and note that Mr Fahy touched in his time here.

KOLLVITZ: You have an Irish Intelligence Service. You have not told me what you hear from them. What do they suspect? We are fighting a war, we have fought two wars with the British in the last thirty years. We take this matter very seriously.

O'KANE: We've been fighting the Brits since 1798.

KOLLVITZ: Understand clearly the delicate balance of our relationship. There are other more serious intelligence organisations, as I know you know, operations that could be dangerous for you at a personal level.

O'KANE: Surely to God not a threat, Volker?

KOLLVITZ: Realpolitik. I will allow you some information. Your phone has been tapped.

MALLIN: And?

KOLLVITZ: You have received calls from inside our country.

O'KANE: Calls?

KOLLVITZ: Undesirables.

O'KANE: What undesirables?

KOLLVITZ: I don't know what other agencies are declaring as undesirables. All I know is that others are monitoring your legation and similar neutral representatives here in Berlin.

O'KANE: Overheard calls so our answers would be overheard? Volker, we have absolutely nothing to hide.

KOLLVITZ: Be careful is what I am saying.

O'KANE: You've been visiting here a few times after we've gone for the evening?

KOLLVITZ: Your excellent cook welcomes me. I assume you have no problem with that?

MALLIN: No. And we thank you for the generous food gifts.

O'KANE: We were getting a little tired of the bread and bratwurst and the coffee ersatz.

KOLLVITZ: Really you should be supplied from the fine products of your own country.

O'KANE has poured himself a glass of wine.

O'KANE: The night fishing boats that ply Cork to Cherbourg and bring the diplomatic bag, I believe they're pleased to do that for pennies and patriotism, but they might draw the line at shunting loin of lamb and Kerry butter. It might also weigh down their little boats when the Royal Navy pursues them.

KOLLVITZ: You will not have a problem with my arranging food for your cook. It is entirely my pleasure, as long as we remain friends.

KOLLVITZ raises his glass in a toast.

To friendship.

O'KANE: Sláinte…

MALLIN, O'KANE, gather coats etc. to leave.

MALLIN: Do you know if they've cleared the bomb damage from Wilhemstrasse?

KOLLVITZ: It's open again. No problems there.

O'KANE: Guten nacht.

KOLLVITZ: Guten nacht.

They go.

For a moment KOLLVITZ is alone in the office. He goes to O'KANE's desk, looks at some of the papers, then over to the chest where O'KANE and MALLIN have been tossing the Fahy papers in for shipment to Dublin. Then he calls out.

Fraulein Moller.

A pause and then she enters.

Sit down.

CHRISTE: I have to check the kitchen, the steamed pudding.

KOLLVITZ: That will keep. Whether it steams another hour or not. Sit.

She sits.

First, I want to inform you, if I'm called away after you've cooked for me, and there is this curfew, I'll arrange for one of my men to escort you home.

CHRISTE: Thank you.

KOLLVITZ: Tuesday night. Everything was exceptional. The duck, perfect. Clever that you got the breast crisp and yet the meat delicate. And you still deny you are a professional cook?

CHRISTE: I've only cooked, for a household.

KOLLVITZ: The banker O'Neill's family?

CHRISTE: Yes.

He goes to a drinks tray, pours a glass of Alsace, offers it to her.

KOLLVITZ: I know so little about you. What did your papa do for his work? Yes?

CHRISTE: A cashier.

KOLLVITZ: He was a cashier, where?

CHRISTE: In a bank.

KOLLVITZ: What bank?

CHRISTE: The Dresdner.

KOLLVITZ: And your mother?

CHRISTE: She was a housewife.

KOLLVITZ: And I think you have a brother?

Reaction CHRISTE.

CHRISTE: A student.

KOLLVITZ: What age is your brother now?

CHRISTE: Thirty something.

KOLLVITZ: Thirty something? You don't reveal much about yourself and your family. Are there secrets? I'm so proud to speak of mine. My father, a farmer, poor until the new dawn and now organised, mechanised, important to his community in Coburg. My mother, now dead, was a servant girl. She loved cooking and food, but she was just a servant until my father's position improved. There is a story to tell you about my mother. The chef in the kitchens at Nordstrand accused her of stealing some foie gras and beat her, beat her badly. Years pass but she does not forget the chef's name – Mainz. So now when I have my position I decide to investigate Herr Mainz. And what do I find – a little of the Jew in the gentleman's family, a grandmother, one of that race. Sadly my mater is already passed away when I have this man for questioning. You should have seen his face. Not even he knew his tainted blood. Well he has now gone to a place where he will no longer have to protect the safety of a rich man's foie gras. Where he is sent he will not be encountering one gram of foie gras. But I'm more interested in your people. Tell me more about your brother.

CHRISTE: I haven't seen him for years.

KOLLVITZ: Years? You know a meal I once had in Cologne? The three duck in a dish. Roast duck breast, then a sausage made from neck and leg, and a pate from duck livers.

CHRISTE: It sounds…very fine.

KOLLVITZ: Your father was a cashier you say. He was in fact a bank manager. You never mentioned your brother went to prison for political acts.

CHRISTE: He was very young. Our Leader went to prison for political acts.

KOLLVITZ: I suggest, very different from your brother's. Your father's a bank manager. Dresdner was a Jew bank. Not any longer. You see that is what is great about our nation. The business that gives us the wealth of power, enfranchised. Taken from those only interested in their own profit and given to everyone. Enfranchised. That word. Everything, everyone enfranchised. My papa, a bankrupt small man, helped by the state to start again. And prosper. Fifteen years ago he would have had no voice in our nation. I would have had no voice, the pauper son of a bankrupt farmer, with no education and no prospects. But the cost of all this is what we must call 'balance'. Hard decisions, sometimes frightening ones, cutting out the cancer of those who are against the general good of our nation. Balance. Not to go too far in this, against not to go far enough. Do we always get the balance right? There's a question for you. Do you think we get it right. Yes?

CHRISTE: I suppose so.

KOLLVITZ: The balance has to be said as, 'the best that we can do' and mistakes few. Is that a good rallying cry? Come on…?

CHRISTE: Yes.

KOLLVITZ: I never asked. How did you get your employment here? You were working for the O'Neill family.

CHRISTE: Mr O'Neill recommended me.

KOLLVITZ: Before he closed the bank and went back to Ireland.

CHRISTE: Yes.

KOLLVITZ: So unnecessary to close the bank. Some in our business circles over here find it unfortunate that this small threat of air raids should cause a retreat from our Capital. Important English banks, like Barclays, are still trading in places, of course with different personnel.

CHRISTE: I think Mr O'Neill wanted to take his sons back to Ireland for their education.

KOLLVITZ: Better than our nation's schools? Hard to believe that.

CHRISTE: I don't know.

KOLLVITZ: I asked for your personnel file from Herr Mallin. You were a year into the study of languages at Dortmund Gymnasium. Then you left. Why?

CHRISTE: I had no money to continue.

KOLLVITZ: No support? No family?

CHRISTE: No one could support me.

KOLLVITZ: Tell me more about your brother. When did you last meet?

CHRISTE: It's…years. (*Pause.*) Maybe two years. I saw him on Lutzow Strasse. We exchanged a few words, only. We were never close.

KOLLVITZ: Curious. When parents die young, siblings are close. You see, I'm interested in you. So I learn things. I discover the sad news of your parents dead in a car crash,

Christmas '32. You would have been very young. Eleven? Twelve?

CHRISTE nods.

Who brought you up – not your brother?

CHRISTE: An aunt.

KOLLVITZ: In Hamburg?

CHRISTE: Yes.

KOLLVITZ: Don't you find it a very curious place, Hamburg? So many strange ideas, strange faces. Black Africans from our adventures in Empire. Seamen from China. And why were there so many Roma? And of course, the Jews. And worse than the Jews, Communists. The Communists we have failed since Weimar days to ferret out. You are still a good Roman creed Catholic?

CHRISTE: Yes.

KOLLVITZ: Church on Sunday, fish on Friday and your Lenten wage to Peter's Pence. I am a Lutheran but I know about Catholics. When did you become a Catholic Christe?

CHRISTE: When?

KOLLVITZ: Not a lot of Catholics in Hamburg. Immigrants, Communists, Jews, yes. Catholics, a very small minority. Useful to you to be a Catholic for employment with the O'Neill family. You could take their boys to church and teach them clear thoughts and to practice their catechisms. And then of course for you to get employment here in this Ireland legation. When did you kneel to a priest and become a Catholic?

CHRISTE: Four years ago.

KOLLVITZ: You were not a Catholic, and then you were?

CHRISTE: Yes.

KOLLVITZ: You're a very truthful person. I ask you questions and you answer correctly. So when did you last talk to your brother?

CHRISTE: I told you, about two years ago.

KOLLVITZ: Two years since you spoke.

CHRISTE: Yes.

KOLLVITZ: Curious. I ask you questions but you never ask me anything. Like why am I interested so much in your fine cooking. Ask me.

CHRISTE: Please tell me.

KOLLVITZ: Before I became involved in my present work what do you think I did?

CHRISTE: I don't know.

KOLLVITZ: To know you would have to walk into the dining room of the Grand Kempinski Hotel where I would greet you. Because I was the maître d' there. Until four years ago when the call of our Leader was more important than chaperoning rich bankers and socialites and Jews to their tables and seeing them so comfortably wined and dined. A famous chef, French, Monsieur Gilles Moretta, he was the star there. I've not tasted finer food than those dishes he gracefully prepared for the staff. You are not a Monsieur Moretta but you are almost as good. One of his signature dishes was breast of duck with various capers and herbs. Yours would be a fine match.

CHRISTE: Thank you.

KOLLVITZ: So one of the few pleasures of my present occupation is access to certain people, not black marketeers, but people who know where a Berliner can still find the best. It's a pleasure to bring such food to your kitchen here.

CHRISTE: Thank you.

KOLLVITZ: Is our dinner nearly ready?

CHRISTE: Yes. If you will please excuse me I will serve it shortly.

KOLLVITZ: That duck the other night I think was finer than the ones made by chef Moretta. I will say I've not tasted such a meal since I holidayed once in Warsaw. It's a dish sometimes found there. So popular in certain restaurants, in the Jewish quarter.

To black.

The next morning.

MALLIN at his desk. CHRISTE brings in coffee. Pours for MALLIN.

MALLIN: Thank you. Did the air raid worry you?

CHRISTE: No. But it was quite close to here.

MALLIN: Well don't concern yourself too much. British bombers getting lucky, somehow dodging around our air defences. But you can imagine the government isn't going to allow its capital city to be pummelled. They'll be beefing up our searchlights and guns. Have yourself a coffee. And sit down.

She pours a cup and sits. He continues to read Fahy papers.

CHRISTE: Herr Mallin.

MALLIN: Yes?

CHRISTE: I wanted to ask you for some advice.

MALLIN: Certainly.

CHRISTE: I have a friend. She is worried, for herself, for her family. She is completely honest, not in trouble with the authorities. But the bombing, and the problems with employment now. So many questions asked.

MALLIN: So?

CHRISTE: She wants to know about the borders. You are a diplomat, do you know if it's possible to go to Austria and then on into Switzerland.

MALLIN: I would say that any problem would be with Switzerland. It's a neutral country protecting its borders and its people. Why would it want Germans leaving their own country because they did not feel safe? I for one would feel as safe here as anywhere.

CHRISTE: The friend has heard there are many places in Austria where you can just walk across the border. Have you heard that?

MALLIN: That would be illegal.

CHRISTE: She says there are organisations, secret ones, in Switzerland that would help people who are…well, worried about living in Germany.

MALLIN: If you follow the laws here, there is nothing to worry about. And I can tell you this war is succeeding. The bombers from the RAF will soon be seen off.

CHRISTE: All my friend simply wants to know is can you travel easily through Austria to the Swiss border, are there new problems on the Austrian side of Switzerland? I said you would know.

MALLIN: Well I don't. I honestly don't.

CHRISTE: I said I'd try to find out from you.

MALLIN: So your friend who's worried about herself and her family for no good reason wants to know if she can enter Switzerland illegally?

CHRISTE: She mentioned it as a possibility to me. Of course, in confidence.

Pause.

MALLIN: This friend, unnamed, are you, by any stroke, talking about yourself, Christe?

CHRISTE: No.

MALLIN: Sure?

CHRISTE: Yes.

MALLIN: You're a good person – a good worker. This is a fine country at war and one that it will win. I'd keep a distance from any friend of yours who wants to do anything illegal. Yes?

CHRISTE: Yes, Herr Mallin.

She goes out. MALLIN looks after her, thoughtful.

O'KANE passes and greets CHRISTE. Enters on MALLIN.

O'KANE: I'm becoming an old man. Me balls are drying out. No longer two ripe plums but a pair of brass buttons rattling the groin. I see a strap of a woman walk by and I wouldn't concede to have the leg off her unless drink taken. Me dreams are nightmare scruting between the ideas of the man I was and the gobshite this graceless job in this bastard city has made of me.

MALLIN: (*Firm.*) Keep quiet.

O'KANE: Why? I was a fool charmin' joxer in my life's prime so recent. A dab hand at the ladies, those of birth and your back street streels. Now, for an instance, that shofure we use when the lad can party some petroleum. Last Thorsday, he and I to a bierkeller on the half street, Motzstrade what hasn't given way to Brit bombs. I met a tart there. Alpine breastworks, soft face, high earner. But she says she'll charge me nothing save what's left of me packet of Sweet Afton. But could I get the bladed devil to rise from depth? No, he stayed home. This sodding war has made me feckin impotent.

MALLIN: If it had made you dumb it would have been worth it. Tell me something.

Why do you go out with whores – spend money on them? Surely there are women about that are not just cash registers?

O'KANE: You want an answer?

MALLIN: Yes.

O'KANE: I'm timid of the love of a woman. You want the truth? I've loved and lost. Really loved and really lost. And that hurts. So what does a joxer with a few drinks taken need on a lonely night? A few minutes of houghmagandie to make the blade happy and to have a sleep of the just.

MALLIN: So a whore is just a receptacle like gaining relief by using your blade to evacuate into a toilet?

O'KANE: Crude, but a fair summation.

MALLIN: You're disgusting.

MALLIN, reading, reacts.

O'KANE: You look as if you've found an item.

MALLIN: Two.

O'KANE: Am I to hold the breath long?

MALLIN: So it's an obvious point we've missed. Where did Fahy get his travelling money from?

O'KANE: God knows.

MALLIN: (*Indicates a book.*) His diary. Showing his journeys. One in only five booked through our agent. He was not a man of family cash, trusts, like you, private income. So times to Geneva, nine in two years. Twice to Norway. Three times to France, Vichy. Twice to Italy.

O'KANE: You were colleague to him at this address over three years and now you discover he was often on the tour.

MALLIN: He took his holidays as he was entitled. I didn't know, I never asked, where he went.

O'KANE: Maybe he was in with a rich travelling lady. I've never been kept myself but I'm told it's one means of exotic travel.

MALLIN: He never mentioned a lady.

O'KANE: So quiet men make spies?

MALLIN: This. A journey to Stebbenreich. That was the Storm troopers' HQ for the elite. The head man, Rohm assassinated.

O'KANE: But for that reason wouldn't a lot of old SA people be against Herr Adolphus and his current lot and may be ready to help the Brits?

MALLIN: You're a bit more clued up than you give away.

O'KANE: You have to be clued up around here pal. If you're a civilian it can be here today, gone tomorrow. Like I'm talking about work camps and concentration camps. I've been ever on the point of asking Kollvitz what his views are on Bergen Belsen, what exactly he thinks of what is going on there.

MALLIN: Don't you dare.

O'KANE: Why not?

MALLIN: Our hosts' internal security is not our business.

O'KANE: You know well they're disappearing Jews and others.

MALLIN: I'm not listening.

O'KANE: No listening, so not hearing, nor seeing. What constitutes courage? The ability to make a courageous decision, like saying to Kollvitz what is your mob doing at Bergen Belsen. Courage equals sensitivity, to be fully sensitive to an issue. Two, hardness, to have the backbone for statement or action. Three injustice, you can't take living with a foul situation any more, four, temper, courage can be entirely losing your rag. Five, evolution. You can no longer deny man has evolved to the point where he can make an exact humanist decision.

MALLIN ignores him, reading.

So I've got an acronym, you see. For courage…sensitivity, right? Hardness, injustice, temper, evolution. S.H.I.T.E. 'Shite.' Bergen Belsen. Do you and I have SHITE Mallin? I'm thinking of a very specific.

MALLIN: I'm not listening.

O'KANE: The fact that we're pals with these Hun and we have not the courage, the guts, to take them up on this business. Thousands disappearing.

MALLIN: Who says it's the fact? Thousands is propaganda. Communist propaganda, Russian Communist propaganda.

O'KANE: You know that's bullshit.

MALLIN: I know this is not any business of the Republic of Ireland's legation in Berlin. Besides you as a Holy Roman will know your Pope, all the top boys here in Germany, are Catholics. Your Pope would put a stop to it.

O'KANE: He's one of them.

MALLIN: What?

O'KANE: He's one of them. I mean it. By his silence.

MALLIN: Diplomats don't go accusing their host country of killing its citizens.

O'KANE: Why not?

MALLIN: The reasons we are here – to promulgate trade, to protect such of our citizens that are in the Fatherland, and to have some knowledge of our German hosts, and contacts, when they become the rulers of Europe.

O'KANE: You think they're going to be that?

MALLIN: It's the best bet out there.

O'KANE: You know the Russians – they've just encircled Von Paulus' Sixth Army at Stalingrad? And you've heard about El Alamein?

MALLIN: Yes so?

O'KANE: D'you know what remains of Genoa and Danzig after the British bombers visited? Dust. And of course, Cologne. We don't talk about that. The Brits left a bit of cathedral, right? So funerals could be conducted for an entire city.

MALLIN just glares at him. O'KANE goes on reading.

(*Muses.*) Bergen Belsen.

MALLIN: Bergen is only eighty miles from here. The Communists are saying thousands are starving and dying there. Find a witness. There must be real and proper witnesses who can say 'Oh yes, I've seen it.' One reliable witness who's not a Communist, a fellow traveller, an enemy of these Axis powers, someone who reliably saw these folks destroyed.

O'KANE: You know there are reports from escapees for Christ sake! You know that.

MALLIN: Who are they? Who's not to say they're agitators, lunatics, they're in there because they've got more than a grudge against the state.

O'KANE: The Polish cardinals have talked to the Pope. The cardinals have told the Pope our hosts are disposing by death and disease numbers of Jews. The Pope does nothing. So the Polish cardinals have told leading churchmen in Norway. The Norwegians are getting the information out to the rest of the world. All these people are dumb, lying, propagandists? I'm feeling my conscience rising like a Hell of a phoenix!

MALLIN: If that's your contribution to our work here, you should seriously consider going home.

O'KANE: God, wouldn't that be wonderful. Let me think about it.

CHRISTE enters with duster.

MALLIN: Miss Moller.

CHRISTE: Yes?

MALLIN: Kapitan Von Kollwitz phoned. He's coming by. Again, this is a legation, a privacy of the Irish people, accessible solely by invitation to foreign nationals, uniquely on business or passport or legal affairs. So this business of, he comes up, brings food, you cook for him…

O'KANE: Miss Moller, are you somewhat having an affair with this Kapitan?

CHRISTE: No. No!

O'KANE: I say be careful. Kollvitz is not necessarily what he seems. You'd do well to be very careful.

MALLIN: (*To O'KANE.*) Stay to the point. Miss Moller, is there any other reason why this man visits you, apart from your cooking?

She pauses.

O'KANE: Yes…?

CHRISTE: Well, perhaps… He's…he's lonely.

MALLIN: Your father was German but your mother was Polish. So you told us. An officer, a German officer would have access to knowledge of your background and he would not be attracted to the Polish part of you. The party, that includes the Security Service, do not, as different from us, like Poles. You tell us after each time he comes exactly what he says or does or asks. And don't fool yourself. This person might be after much richer fare than a meal.

O'KANE: Don't talk like that you silly man. Christe is old enough to look after herself.

MALLIN: Don't criticise me in front of staff.

O'KANE: Staff? A word on plurality. There's you, me and Christe. She is hardly staff. Say 'Will you not criticise me in front of Christe.' (*To CHRISTE.*) You can go dear.

She leaves.

MALLIN: You'll try me to the limit. We need to know if Kollvitz wants to get cook to talk about Fahy.

O'KANE: Fahy's gone. Back to the city of God, holding up the bar in Nearys, trailing porter pissed on boots across the dunes of College Green, cracking some dirty joke with the Archbishop in bona fides, haranguing some Brit shite visitor in the Shelbourne lobby, smoking the Sweet Afton which should be ours by rights if we could ever get a diplomatic bag sent here to the capital of blitzkreig, a blitzkreig that seems now to be going the other way. That reminds me.

He goes to side table pours himself a glass of wine.

MALLIN: It's five thirty in the afternoon.

O'KANE: That's where you're wrong. Sun over the yard arm. It's five thirty in the evening. D'you think it's at all possible that Fahy working here in the capital might have been responsible for getting some of these facts about Bergen Belsen out to the wide world?

MALLIN: Be early tomorrow. This chest must go off to Dublin soon.

O'KANE: I'll do me best, no better than that. You know Mallin, there's just two of us, both of the auld sod, both university men, we should try to get on better with each other. Forgive and forget, join hands, look after each other, be pals.

MALLIN: We can be pals if you stop being so infantile. Do your work. Act reasonably. Just stop taking the piss, alright?

O'KANE: Alright.

He's standing near the radio which has been on low volume. The Reich national anthem starts up. O'KANE turns the volume up.

Mallin, have you ever tap danced to Deutschland Uber Alles?

O'KANE starts tap dancing a four beat to the anthem swinging his arms around.

MALLIN, angry, strides out.

O'KANE finishes tap dance, grabs his coat, dances with it a minute, then goes out.

To black.

Up on CHRISTE and KOLLVITZ at table. Night. They have just finished the meal CHRISTE cooked.

KOLLVITZ: A brilliant meal. But I anticipated no less. To greater appreciate tonight I deliberately missed lunch today. In fact I went to visit my neighbour, his wife and son. It was the son's birthday. Six years. A beautiful young boy. And of course he calls me 'uncle'. I'm not his uncle but that's what he says. And he runs to me and I lift him up into my arms and he laughs and kisses me. When I see a young boy like that I'm full of pride. They are our future. Our future is in good hands. You like children?

CHRISTE: Yes, of course.

KOLLVITZ: Do you have cousins?

CHRISTE: Both my parents had no siblings.

KOLLVITZ: That's an answer which would give you no relatives but you have this brother. Does he have children?

CHRISTE: No.

KOLLVITZ: And you don't see him?

CHRISTE: I don't.

KOLLVITZ: You're younger than me – maybe ten years? That's not a decade, it's a lifetime. In the Reich, just ten years is an epoch, a history renewed. From a million marks for a loaf of bread to prosperity, not for the few, not for bankers or bourgeoisie, but for everyone. This year, 1942, will see those events that turn this war to our victory, across every corner of this continent. I'm not an educated man, but I believe I had a better education not from books or professors but from the wisdom of our Leader. He has told me there is only one solution for all of us to succeed, the hard choice. Discipline ourselves and seek out our enemies. Those who undermine, try to destroy our great vision. You agree?

CHRISTE: Yes.

KOLLVITZ: How can we still have these problems, even in this capital city. The enemy within. Why am I not fighting in the East or in Africa. Ask me why? (*Emphasis.*) Ask me.

CHRISTE: Yes?

KOLLVITZ: Because I am ordered into the front line of a battle in our Homeland as brutal and murderous as any faced by our Panzers in Russia or the heroes of Afrika Corps. Have you met my enemies? Do you know my enemies?

CHRISTE: I don't understand.

KOLLVITZ: Do you believe the lunatics who voted for a Communist government here in Berlin twenty years ago have gone away? The Jews we can deal with. Our people who are treacherous Communists are another problem. You walk down the street in Prenzlauer. You see two men talking quietly together. They are not Jews, you pass them by. They are worse. Communists. They want to destroy us and annex our civilisation to Russia, a race of subhumans, slaves. I was to go into the army. My father said this is now a nation worth dying for. He didn't say worth fighting for, but worth dying for. So I did my training in a barracks in Steglitz. Then one night, late at night, the sergeant came into our hut and said some Jews had been found by our men hiding in a farm two kilometres away, and were there volunteers to deal with them. I was the first. That quality was noticed. I was promoted from a soldier to State Security. You see I also found out the farmer who sheltered the Jews was a Communist. I had gone back alone the next day and executed him. A million marks for a loaf of bread. People dying of starvation. A civilisation in slavery to the Treaty of Versailles. And then came a leader who brought us from chaos to prosperity, and work for everyone. How can there be traitors to his vision and his acts? It beggars belief. Can you think of other reasons I come here?

CHRISTE: You like my cooking.

KOLLVITZ: There is something else. I wonder when I will tell you what it is. You're an attractive woman. It's a time of war. Berlin can be a lonely place. You are an interesting woman, of mystery… So your employers, where are they tonight? The young one O'Kane is trawling for drink and prostitutes. Mallin, the severe one, is at a lecture at the Kuntsler Institute. And we are alone. Take your jacket coat off.

A long hesitation. She does.

Now sit down, Christe.

He goes to a drinks tray.

Drink?

CHRISTE: I don't drink.

KOLLVITZ: A small Irish whisky which you will drink.

He pours and offers the glass. He waits while she drinks it.

A woman of mystery. Born Hamburg, worked for an Irishman. That gave you a certain 'in', at this legation. 'I need a job. I was employed by an Irishman.' Did they really think about who you were, not who you said you were? Your employers here are generous. Generous. The first time I tasted your cooking I knew. The cooking of a Jewess. It's hot for the city this autumn. It's hot in here. Undo the buttons on your blouse. You do know who I am. I too live a mystery. Your employers would say I am from the Foreign Ministry but you, a Jewess, will know who I work for. At first it was difficult to find the true details, births and deaths. Parents. One record office destroyed by bombing. But there were other ways. I am not interested in you, but your brother. The Communist. The agitator. I'm interested that you lied about his existence. There are obvious reasons why you did lie.

CHRISTE: No.

KOLLVITZ: People say you were very close to him. They say that.

CHRISTE: No.

KOLLVITZ goes to his briefcase. He takes out his Leica camera.

KOLLVITZ: Expose your breasts now. Do it.

There's a long hesitation. KOLLVITZ waits patiently. But she knows she is defeated. She takes off her blouse and bra.

Fraulein Christe, you know the power I have. I can exercise it here gently, or at our headquarters, harshly. You've heard, as a Jewess, all the stories.

He begins to take photos.

You know you're quite beautiful. Such a waste. A beautiful body wasted on a Jewess. We know your brother is moving around from one place to another. He's clever. Perhaps he doesn't say to you where he is. But you'll find out for us. We have hesitated so far to arrest you. Two reasons. You could be useful to us here. And also it might cause a small diplomatic incident. We need a friendly Republic of Ireland for our new Europe. We wish to turn the tables of history. For years the British have persecuted the people of Ireland. Now these Irish will likely be the new masters of England. There will be much irony in the new order when this war is over. Remove your dress. Then sit on the edge of the desk. Do it!

She continues to strip until she is naked.

KOLLVITZ puts the camera aside and moves towards her, stops. She rises and moves towards him.

To black.

End of Act One.

Act Two

MALLIN enters from street. O'KANE is back sorting papers, crosses to tea chest, drops some in.

MALLIN: Anything to report?

O'KANE: Not a lot.

MALLIN: What?

O'KANE: Some eejit lost his passport, or it was stolen from him.

MALLIN: 'Eejit'?

O'KANE: At 130 Wilhelmshaven Strasse, basement and first three floors.

MALLIN: Why the specific address?

O'KANE: God you've led a sheltered life. It's the biggest brothel in Berlin.

MALLIN: He contacts the polizei. He comes in, fills out the form.

O'KANE: He doesn't.

MALLIN: Doesn't?

O'KANE: No forms.

MALLIN: No forms?! That's your responsibility...

O'KANE: Jesus man, your responsibility is to know we ran out – those and passport blanks. All we've got is the little yoke of the official stamp.

MALLIN: How could we run out?

O'KANE: Ask the man in the street, there's a war on. I put in a docket six weeks back for your forms, your blanks and also five hundred Sweet Afton, some soap, a half dozen of the socks...

MALLIN: Stick to the point.

O'KANE: The man who lost his passport. He gave me his name – McCleary, Bernard. He kept saying, 'Do you know who I am?' I said the Devil I didn't.

MALLIN: So who is he?

O'KANE: He said he was that McCleary, chairman and specialist with the Irish Veterinary Association, heading for Frankfurt and Main to advise on some outbreak of foot and mouth. He certainly was an expert on the mouth.

MALLIN: Radio Dublin, get forms, blanks put on a fisher boat urgent. This is ludicrous. We can't replace a passport! Did he leave a contact number?

O'KANE: He did.

MALLIN: Phone him to report here in two or three days. I mean he may be important.

O'KANE: I don't know if they have phones where he is.

MALLIN: Where?

O'KANE: Jail.

MALLIN: Jail?

O'KANE: He, and a very temporary lady friend had been found drunk and extremely disorderly. You wouldn't know this, but drink is taken in these brothels.

MALLIN: Don't be stupid and flippant.

O'KANE: I'm educating you. It's sexual congress plus alcohol – equally why men go to Whilhelmshaven Street. He kept saying, in his drink-taken way, 'don't you know who I am?' I said…

MALLIN: Well?

O'KANE: I said d'you think it's because I haven't made a note of your name, or because you think you're somebody important? And he said, 'I am very important as you will find out,' said he.

MALLIN: (*Shrugs.*) Chairman, Irish Veterinary Association, I don't think so. Get him a lawyer.

O'KANE: Maybe two.

MALLIN: (*Weary.*) What?

O'KANE: Ah, when he was arrested he was missing the pantaloons, the pair, both legs.

MALLIN: What?!

O'KANE: Though I'm told a typical Tipperary man will approach his lovemaking without the trousers but with his overcoat and boots fully on and often in the company of his favourite milker.

MALLIN: I have truly had enough of you!

O'KANE: The facts are these. On his arrest in the strasse he had no lower garment. Full display of hairy legs and maybe the bits between, though he did not mention a charge of indecency.

MALLIN: Christ!

O'KANE: So do you think we should maybe offer, with a cheque to be refunded by the veterinary crowd, a pair of cords, reasonably quality, but well cut. It's very embarrassing having no trousers about you in a foreign clink. I suggest our best considered course of action is to do damn all. The polizei will likely wait for him to sober up and then toss him out in the street. He can go back to the brothel for three days till we have the passport for him. Fair enough?

MALLIN: How dare people come to Berlin and behave like that, letting down our country.

O'KANE: Agreed. Dreadful. Wicked. Trouserless.

MALLIN: God almighty…

MALLIN is now at his desk, starts reading Fahy's papers. Long pause.

O'KANE: Did you ever meet your man, Dev?

MALLIN: I'm warning you!

O'KANE: I'm allowed to speak you know. It's in our constitution. You don't have to hear.

MALLIN: Do you ever think that there were boys, fifteen to eighteen, boys, some still in school who fought in the Uprising? Do you think the young men who offered their lives for the future of our country would have been impressed by your so-called fucking humour and whoring as the representative of their nation just twenty four years later?

O'KANE: You're a serious mon, Derry, a little too lost in the past. It wasn't that great was it?

MALLIN: You're beyond help.

MALLIN is reading Fahy's papers. Silence then.

O'KANE: I am allowed to converse you know. I'm no member of the Silent Orders, monks nor nuns. And you'll learn from me. I've met him several times. The great leader, Dev.

MALLIN ignores.

He had such a history. But not a handsome lad. Fair haired, wall-eyed, suffering from teeth broke well below the gumline, and with freckles to ape florins on both saggy buttocks. A tall man, short in appearance, he had joined the African Navy and had in his dismasted frigate done deeds of great warfare in several pitched battles on treacherous seas deep in the Sahara. Latter-day he came to Ireland to apply as a senior inspector of tickets on the Dalkey tram, a post he failed to secure. So he turned his focus to politics. There seemed to be a living had in it for a joxer with no misgivings about a few soiled notes passed underhand by those seeking preferments.

MALLIN: When are you going to stop this?

O'KANE: For an Irish lad he was a great American, a private
levity which had saved him from his facing the firing squad
after he went to the wrong post office to send a parcel of
oxtails to Finglas. The lack of bullets in his crucial cavities
expressed this person in the nation's mind as being at once
a coward and equally a hero, at least to the congregation in
Nearys bar…

MALLIN: Can you finish, at least for a few seconds? Why
does Kollvitz want you to visit some industrial site? What
industrial site?

O'KANE: I think he reads our reports home.

MALLIN: Impossible, scrambled and encoded.

O'KANE: He knows I'm more of the dab hand at the words
than you. I can make literature out of a train timetable.
Try me.

MALLIN: Answer the question. Why you?

O'KANE: Don't know. I was chatting to him, asked him
sort of vague, how about the recent bombs and the war
production around Berlin, factories for guns, planes, of that
manner – hadn't they all been flattened. He said not a whit
of it, and he would put me in his motorcar and we would
tour some factories and see how bombing has changed
nothing.

MALLIN: I don't see the point.

O'KANE: The point is I write reports home so our leaders
know the German nation is still much in business, and not
to think about maybe it might be worth Old Ireland to start
finagling with the Brits.

MALLIN: He's going to pick you up and drive you around
factories?

O'KANE: He is.

MALLIN: Doesn't seem right. These boys are tight lipped about bomb damage. No one know its effect. There's nothing in the papers. No one in diplomatic circles that I've heard, knows anything. Why would Kollvitz take a minor official to see factories functioning?

O'KANE: Less of the 'minor official' pal, friendly official of the legation of a much loved country.

MALLIN: You be careful. We're not completely clear about Kollvitz's work and his position. I don't know who or what he represents.

O'KANE: There's nothing about Herr Kollvitz that we can't handle.

MALLIN: You may rue those words.

They read. A pause.

O'KANE: I've decided to be honest with you, just the once mind.

MALLIN: Look. Cut your gab!

O'KANE: I'm not going to tell you how I joined the Diplomatic Service, but why I'm here, in Berlin town.

MALLIN: Don't.

O'KANE: You must know. In case I ask you for the urgent loan of a fold of Deutschmarks.

MALLIN: I'll lend you nothing.

O'KANE: You'll lend to save my life.

MALLIN: Fuck you I wouldn't.

O'KANE: It began at the beginning, back with the familiar Dev and my dada…

MALLIN: I'm no longer listening to you.

O'KANE: 'There's a problem with me lad,' says me dad, scrutin' Eamonn Dev the Leery, 'it's a crime that's much worse than the bayonet sodomy of the Tans and Blacks back in the good auld days. It is worse than thieving a widow of her last small grotes. It is a border crossing that once crossed there's no return. It's the black moon that would spark the lightning that could kill a pope. It is a sin as dark as the darkest part of the bride's crossed legs. It is infamy.'

'So what,' says the Dev, 'is it with your boyo? What infamy?'

'He is a gambler. He'll have the bet on anything. How often you launder your drawers? Whether some castrato has no bollocks or one, retaining that for fatherhood in case of a career change. He'll make a bet on how many moths on your great coat, or whether your whore will have twins…'

MALLIN: It never occurred to you why bookies are rich?

O'KANE: Okay. Latterly.

MALLIN: So you've left bad debts back home.

O'KANE: Sadly. Jawhol.

MALLIN: How much?

O'KANE: Enough to buy a farm, a bull with hot bollocks, and say five score of milkers.

MALLIN: Thousands of pounds?

O'KANE: Yes.

MALLIN: Have you run up debts here? Your night life? You've been to horse races as well, yes?

O'KANE: A few.

MALLIN: Fahy was another idiot who bet on horses.

O'KANE: It's a popular sport.

MALLIN: Will you have creditors knocking on this door?

O'KANE: Not probably.

MALLIN: Meaning what?

O'KANE: So far, so far I've run up no serious debts.

MALLIN: Define 'serious'.

O'KANE: Nothing I can't handle. And of course, if Bielefeldt is anything to go by, both myself and those owed may be cancelled by the Brit bombers.

MALLIN: You're seriously telling me you had debt problems in Dublin and you've run up credit here?

O'KANE: Just in case there's a knock on the door.

MALLIN: I bloody well don't believe it.

O'KANE: I wasn't to know my nice whore had an ace accountant for a pimp and the bar bill had to be paid before Victory in Europe Day.

MALLIN: If your creditors come here I'll lead them direct to you.

O'KANE: That's what I thought. But I also thought you should be warned.

MALLIN: You told me you had a generous father, financially.

O'KANE: No longer. The well has finally run dry.

MALLIN: And family trusts?

O'KANE: Them was worn out years back. Would you like to buy my watch? It's a Hamilton. American.

MALLIN: In a town being bombed you've managed to get yourself into money troubles.

O'KANE: I thought you said they were winning the war? This was just fair warning that I might have creditors ringing our doorbell. Don't worry. I've handled such before.

MALLIN: I'm contacting Dublin. I want you out of here.

O'KANE: Dear old Mallin, they know it all. You write to them by all means. But these things are the reason they want

me here, not there. Look, treat me like you treat the mad
men who run this country. When you judge me, be, like,
neutral.

MALLIN gets up, heads to coat stand, takes coat, walks out.

To black.

*Up on, O'KANE slumped at desk. He reads a German racing paper.
He gets up at the sound of KOLLVITZ entering.*

O'KANE: Volker. How's it hanging?

KOLLVITZ: You are maybe weary of me always arriving? I like
to stop by on the way to my office. To see your progress on
Fahy's papers. Where is Herr Mallin?

O'KANE: Italian commercial attaché.

KOLLVITZ: Ah. So nothing so far in Fahy's papers.

O'KANE: Not a mote or jot. You want an ersatz. I made it
meself. It should still be hot.

Indicates tray with coffee pot and cups.

KOLLVITZ: Thank you.

KOLLVITZ pours himself coffee.

O'KANE: Sit yourself.

KOLLVITZ: Yes.

Pause. He drinks. O'KANE pretends to go back to his reading.

It surprises me you did not know Mr Fahy. Did he not
go to the same university as you – the Protestant one in
Dublin city?

O'KANE: He may have been a regular joxer there. I didn't spot
him. To make a bold observation, my pal and I don't at all
understand what you've got on Fahy. And you won't say,
except he was maybe a spy.

KOLLVITZ: Just as you are here, we are there, with our legation in Dublin city. You learn intelligence here, we learn intelligence there. It's inevitable.

O'KANE: Like what?

KOLLVITZ: We are at war with England. There are thousands of Englishmen in Ireland, and so in Dublin. Some of these will work for British Intelligence. Some of these will have money to buy intelligence. Is it impossible that Fahy who has lived and worked in Berlin for three years and made many contacts has information he could market? We also have information gatherers in Dublin who discover Mr Fahy is not a rich man but like some we are familiar with, has weaknesses and tastes beyond his finances.

O'KANE: What would Fahy learn here that he could sell to the English?

KOLLVITZ: He had friends in many places.

O'KANE: There's a Japanese word, 'crapola'. I think you're talking crapola.

KOLLVITZ: We learn that Fahy's father died and left nothing but debts. So Fahy had to live on his Irish consular income. Not so much. And yet he travelled a lot. He seemed to have meetings with quite important people.

O'KANE: Including his rich girlfriend. I believe he had this sort of wench who had capital to her name.

KOLLVITZ: We know of her. She was not rich.

O'KANE: You've done your homework.

KOLLVITZ: 'Homework'? Our intelligence services do not do 'homework' Mr O'Kane.

It's a dark morning. The desk lights and the overhead candelabra flicker and go off.

O'KANE: The third power cut this week. I'm minding it now. I had the geegees and runners all wrote out last Tuesday night. I'm about to phone the bookies. Power cut. No light to see and the phone's dead. Can you tell me who's ever responsible for the juice, that I missed out on a grand two way double plus your actual winner at Rachenshaven?

KOLLVITZ: I'm sure if you were in London Mr O'Kane the lights would be even more difficult. A part called Docklands. There is no light at all. Except from burning buildings.

The lights flicker and come on again.

You see. We only suffer small inconveniences.

O'KANE: For the moment.

KOLLVITZ: The moment will pass. You would not be here in Berlin if you did not think we will win this war. So nothing from Fahy's papers? Tomorrow when I pick you up to show you this factory complex perhaps by then you will have something useful for me.

He finishes his coffee, gets up.

O'KANE: Perhaps. Perhaps not.

KOLLVITZ heads out.

To black.

Up on

The office. Mid morning.

MALLIN at Fahy's papers at the desk. O'KANE eats a sandwich noisily.

O'KANE: You know, sometimes I can be serious, dead serious. Can I talk serious for a moment?

MALLIN: I'm tired, really sick to death of your gab.

O'KANE: I've been thinking about conscience, the courage to make a decision, an epic, maybe life threatening decision. (*He goes to map of Germany on wall. Points.*) Supposing this railway line was a straight line and we were on a train heading West. Berlin, Westermark, Rathenov, Stendal,

Gardelegen, Wolfsburg, Hannover. And supposing we had all the facts – well we do, about what is happening in Bergen Belsen and other work camps.

MALLIN: I'm not listening.

O'KANE: How far along this line do we, as feeling human beings, get off the train and make our protest – and say that we, legates of Ireland will not accept these murders in silence? Do we get off at Westermark or a bit later at Wolfsburg? Just how courageous and conscience driven are we if we leave the decision well late, to Hanover?

MALLIN continues reading.

Is it a question that we can leave it late, to the very last moment, as long as we do make the decision to get off and protest? At what station do we have to alight to be decent, thinking humans? Does conscience expire somewhere along the line because we will ourself to leave it later and later? Work on it. This is not a time in the affairs of legates where we can sit it out on our arses indefinitely.

MALLIN: You think us two, two minor officials of a small country, can speak out, shout out, and make any difference to anything?

O'KANE: I'm not talking about minor officials, I'm talking about two men…

MALLIN: You may soon not be an official, minor or otherwise.

Silence. O'KANE goes back to desk.

I've got something, sort of. Maybe. It seems about fourteen months ago, March, he went to Dortmund with his woman and took these photos. If I'm not mistaken on that airfield in the background the brand new Junkers JU88 Long Range.

O'KANE: I've seen them. They're dirty snaps, right? She unbuttoned and revealing one tit, not the pair. But you could be right. If some bowsy from Kollvitz's gang saw him taking snaps, that's often enough for the black leather brigade.

MALLIN: You won't face it will you – that Fahy may have been a traitor?

O'KANE: You could wonder if it began with his schooling. Maybe he, like me, fell foul of the Jesuit Order. They're the brutes that can bring out the mischief in a child. Lies, every form of lies to avoid the good fathers' beatings. Secret vices? Gambling? How exactly was he fixed for money? Was he always down to loose change?

MALLIN: He mentions his family had not property, were farm tenants in Finglas.

O'KANE: There's shit soil in Finglas. You couldn't grow a scallion larger than a rabbit's turd.

MALLIN: If he was a spy then he would be dead devious to con the service into thinking he was sound. I had two weeks in my immersion with what they call a psychiatric person.

O'KANE: You'd need it.

MALLIN: Why the dumb arse responses? There's only the two of us in this room? You're not impressing anyone.

O'KANE: Derry Mallin, I have to survive you. I'm a long way from home. I'm being bombed. Every air raid siren signals my possible last breath and I go to Hell with you as my companion. How shite is that?

MALLIN: How did you pass the interview with the psychiatric people?

O'KANE: You want to know how I got into the service?

MALLIN: No!

O'KANE: So me dadda was in an airy plane with Dev, and who was the pilot but a drunken Kerryman who deserved to die and did. He tells our two the yoke will soon crash over Mayo as his brain forgot to refuel at Wexford. And now there's one parachute alone. 'Put it on,' me da says to Dev, 'drape yourself. You're a tall gurrier of no weight and I'm a slight fella of no more substance than the widow's rags. Two of us will use the one parachuting. So it went. They jumped with the one and me dad clings on to Dev like baby Jesus to his ma's tits and when they hit the bog, the Dev is cheerful and says to the dad in his Americano, 'Before we get well-pissed back at the home say what favour you ask for saving of myself being destroyed.' My father's quick response, 'I got a young tyke, a right Rodney and dullard. Put him in the Foreign Service away from Ireland, like Berlin. The Rooshins will win the draw and shoot to death every living soul in that dog crap capital…'

MALLIN: Goddamit, have you finished?!

O'KANE: I have.

MALLIN: So where's Christe?

O'KANE: Maybe sleeping after the air raid warnings last night.

MALLIN: (*Looks at watch.*) Sleeping?

O'KANE: I've had it out of her.

MALLIN: What?

O'KANE: Her little apartment on Selvigstrasse. She was near blown out of her brains night before last. She worries the bombers are aimed at the Reichstag and being well fluthered on Scotch malt and such are hitting everything around it in missing the target. Selvigstrasse, a few rods, poles and perches from your parliament building.

MALLIN: So?

O'KANE: I've suggested in future she can sleep the night here.

MALLIN: What? Where here?

O'KANE: We can make up a bed of cushions. She can bring her linen, and sleep the night. She thought this would suit.

MALLIN: This is a legation not a doss house.

O'KANE: They are trying to hit the Reichstag and they're missing. Do you want her blood on your hands? You'll probably only make one decent human decision this year – let this be it. C'mon man, how can it bother anyone if she has her nights here till the worst of this bombing is over?

MALLIN shrugs.

So I'll tell her. This is how it's done. Get off your arse and help me.

MALLIN doesn't move.

Three chairs with cushions...

He takes the cushions from chairs, lines them up on the floor in front of his desk.

Arranged for the night thus. During the day the cushions are returned to their place. Dusk is approaching. So we'll keep the yokes out. Spread this end to end. This greatcoat

Takes a coat off the coat stand.

left by some person unknown and not collected, thus. Sleep guaranteed.

MALLIN: Only for a few days...

O'KANE: By the law of averages those bombers are bound to flatten the Reichstag at some point soon and then they'll turn their attention to Mussolini's Pope or some such. This city's already becoming a mound of second hand bricks, not much left to dismantle. Hey, this could work nicely for us as well. Certainly when I need a quick shut-eye after the heavy carnal night. Or you could take a rest what with the insurmountable burdens of your office. You must feel the great stress of it all, senior partner in a legation. Too much for any one man.

MALLIN: O'Kane, I could enjoy my job here if it wasn't for your insane childlike endless blather.

O'KANE: You mean about the Dev and me da? And I thought you'd die to know about my personal experience of the great man. And I do mean great. He had buttocks that vast he had difficulty getting a forearm around them to wipe his arse, and stomach so overhung he'd have to guess at how far down to go to scratch his tackle. But a beautiful soul, the poetry of him coming out of every orifice, the music of which led every young virgin to mutiny. My dadda loved him and Dev loved the da. Never criticise the lad. He was vacant eyed to both war and peace because he'd seen it all. He would look at this 'emergency' and say, 'Lads this is not our ruckus, nor not our war, let these heathen battle, but we've a superior appointment at Davey Byrnes where the porter flows and the craic is the one and only great fundament of civilisation to be fought over...'

MALLIN: I think you're going mad. And you can't see it.

O'KANE: I think if you grope around the things I say to you Mallin, you'll find bits of truth more than you'd imagined. I have discovered a small window here in Germany that looks into Hell. I'm happy to show it to you. Maybe sometime you should stare through it. Sooner or later you could be forced to. Every man has his thinking soul, none can escape that.

MALLIN: I'm going to the post office.

O'KANE: Don't put stamps on anything before you check the PO is still standing...

MALLIN goes.

Pause.

O'KANE adjusts greatcoat and cushions. Then heads for street door.

Stage empty.

CHRISTE enters, empties wastepaper basket into paper sack. Doorbell goes. She moves to answer it. KOLLVITZ enters.

CHRISTE: Good afternoon, Volker. Can I make you a coffee?

KOLLVITZ opens his briefcase, brings out a document with photo attached.

KOLLVITZ: I require your signature on this form.

CHRISTE: Signature?

KOLLVITZ: That you authenticate this photograph of your brother.

CHRISTE: Brother? Volker, what is this about?

KOLLVITZ: Why are you now calling me by my Christian name. I hardly know you.

CHRISTE: Why are you saying that?

KOLLVITZ: Your signature please. And some answers. These are details about your brother, which will be revealed to a court of our German people. Yes, we are still a nation under the rule of law. And your authorising necessary for a court of law as your communist Jewish brother used many aliases. He was a palpable liar doubtless due to his inheritance of the lying and scheming nature of his race, a talent you also inherited. Sign.

CHRISTE: Volker, I made an understanding with you. I thought we were two people in this city, lonely, and you like myself in obedience to your superiors and their rules. But with a soul and a heart beneath all that. And now you're saying…

KOLLVITZ: I don't wish to hear any of this nonsense. Will you sign this or not?

CHRISTE: How could I be so wrong that we opposites were…

KOLLVITZ: Stop talking madness. You are a cook to a pair of Irishmen and their guests. But you also know elements unforgivable, and my country, not yours, has suffered people like you for too many years. And we will no longer forgive.

CHRISTE: I don't know how you can dismiss what happened last night and just…

KOLLVITZ: I have no idea what you're talking about.

CHRISTE: Why are you lying?

KOLLVITZ: Are you going to sign this right now.

CHRISTE: No.

KOLLVITZ: I'll return and speak to your employers.

He goes.

Pause. O'KANE enters.

O'KANE: I saw Kollvitz going out. What did he want?

CHRISTE says nothing.

You didn't clear the dishes last night. I did most of them.

CHRISTE says nothing.

See, I talked to Mallin. You have now a bed here. Yes?

O'KANE detects that CHRISTE is withdrawn, upset.

Are you alright?

She doesn't answer.

(*Emphasis.*) Are you alright?

She goes out with some dishes. Comes back, takes more. O'KANE studies her.

It may be a fancy of ours but Mallin and me are your employers, and when I ask 'are you alright?' I'd appreciate from an employer's point of view, an answer.

CHRISTE: Yes.

O'KANE: You don't look alright. You look all wrong. How was it with Kollvitz?

She nods.

He breezes in here with some mutton lamb and thinks he owns the place. Are you fed up with his ugly presence?

CHRISTE: No.

O'KANE: Mallin and I enjoy the extras – good bites, enough so we don't have to eat in the evenings. Evenings is sometimes a cause for bad indigestion due to falling bombs when I'm trying to gorge. You don't say much Christe. All you have to do is the nod, and for instance, we could tell Kollvitz to bugger off. Well?

CHRISTE: I don't want to cause trouble.

O'KANE: How can it be 'trouble'?

CHRISTE: I don't want trouble for you.

O'KANE: Look, Kollvitz's mob are just a bunch of policemen without the brains. They get agitated about all sorts of things, but not you. Right?

She doesn't answer.

We can get rid of him. Clear?

She starts to cry.

(*Gently.*) Sit down. What happened? Mallin and me are well aware he fancies you. Did he make a pass at you? Yes or no? Say it.

CHRISTE: Yes.

O'KANE: What? He made a pass? Or worse? Did he force himself on you?

CHRISTE: I don't want to answer.

O'KANE: How the Hell did you let him?

CHRISTE: He can make problems for me.

O'KANE: What? What kind of problems?

CHRISTE: He doesn't say.

O'KANE: Will you please talk intelligently?

CHRISTE: He is interested in my brother. My brother, he says is a Communist, an agitator, a traitor.

O'KANE: Is he?

CHRISTE: They have files to say he is a Communist party member. It's forbidden.

O'KANE: So where is your brother?

CHRISTE: I don't know. They are hunting for him.

O'KANE: And he forced himself on you?

CHRISTE: Please. I don't want to discuss this.

O'KANE: Go back to your apartment. I'll tell Mallin you're ill.

CHRISTE: I don't want Herr Mallin to know this.

O'KANE: Why? He has to.

CHRISTE: Please, no! No!

O'KANE: Okay. For the moment. You go home. We'll talk about this later. Listen Christe, Mallin and me are not without courage, or convictions. Well, forget Mallin. I can handle a piece of shite like Kollvitz. I can really deal with him. Now are you listening to me? I will never abandon you. Count on that. Whatever happens I will never abandon you. Now go…

CHRISTE's still crying. O'KANE makes a move as if to embrace her, to comfort her. But he stops short.

CHRISTE goes out. O'KANE sits down. He's trying to work it out. The problem of KOLLVITZ is growing and has to be dealt with.

To black.

Up on –

Afternoon.

MALLIN enters on O'KANE.

MALLIN: I don't like this bed here, during the day. As you won't, I'll clear it up. You can put it out later.

MALLIN takes up cushions, piles them in the corner, covers them with greatcoat.

O'KANE ignores that. He has an item from the diplomatic mail bag.

O'KANE: Copy of a telex originating from someone in Berlin, via Sweden. It's brief – says – many more Russian prisoners have arrived in Bergen Belsen. Mallin when are we going to protest about what we know is going on and ask for our legation to be withdrawn?

MALLIN: Know your fucking place! How can you not understand?! We are not here to parade our souls. We are nothing more than visa stampers and a post box for information between Germany and Ireland and Ireland and Germany.

O'KANE: Nothing? We are nothing. You may be nothing. I am not nothing.

MALLIN: Stop wasting your breath and my time!

O'KANE: If you add the figures, the information from Rome, Sweden, Poland, the UK and the Yanks, it's tens of thousands of Jews, Gypsies and others have gone into their camps and have not come out alive. And the rumours that they've built more camps in Poland.

MALLIN: I don't know where you get your so-called facts from.

O'KANE: Everywhere. Everyone knows what's going on with the one exception, you. That party at the Swedish consulate. You were there. That head Swede saying he'd got all this information from his pals in Norway, about Jews rounded up, disposed of. Don't you remember? There was that fat gaulieter there arguing with him, but somehow not denying anything.

MALLIN: Do you know how the great lies work? If you say something often enough people will believe it. Churchill on Dunkirk. He turned it into a victory. A victory for the Brits. People in small boats, outstanding courage etc. It was the biggest defeat the British Army ever had.

O'KANE: So?!

MALLIN: Counter intelligence, misinformation, ludicrous propaganda. Yes, there have been arrests, deportations to forced labour, and concentration camps, no doubt on the model of the ones the Brits set up in the Boer War. People, whole families and their children perished. Yes, there are some wicked men running this nation but the core, the bedrock here is a civilised society.

Pause.

O'KANE: You're nuts. You'd like me, wouldn't you, to go home. You could try it on but I don't think you have enough seniority to have me recalled. I joke about it, but my father is close to de Valera. In a sad sort of way, you're fucked.

The phone rings.

MALLIN: Get that phone.

O'KANE crosses to phone, answers it.

O'KANE: (*Into phone.*) Yes? I am he. Mr Bernard O'Leary of veterinary fame? Yes, I remember. They've released you. Surely wondrous news. Did you purchase some pants? They don't fit! Well try pulling them on over your fat head, or get one of your prostitutes to help you. Yes, you heard me. Don't ring here again. Piss off out of Berlin and don't come back.

He slams phone down.

MALLIN: How dare you!

O'KANE: Yeah Derry, I dare. I'm in the mood to tell a few more people to feck off…

MALLIN: I'm definitely writing to Dublin about you.

O'KANE: If you need help with the spelling…

MALLIN: You sicken me..!

KOLLVITZ enters.

Come in.

KOLLVITZ: I'm sorry to call on you without invitation and a second time today.

MALLIN: You know you don't need an invite.

O'KANE: I think you do, Herr Kollvitz. You need permission, yes. Especially for your night visits…

MALLIN: (*To O'KANE.*) What do you think you're you saying? (*To KOLLVITZ.*) Ignore him.

KOLLVITZ: I need permission to call on Fraulein Moller, German citizen, Herr O'Kane?

O'KANE: This address is the territory of the Irish Free State. We will decide who enters it. To put it mildly, our employee does not want you here.

MALLIN: (*To O'KANE.*) Stop this immediately!

O'KANE: (*To MALLIN.*) Fraulein Moller does not welcome this man's presence. I can't say more than that. She's told me not to.

MALLIN: I don't believe this! What has she told you?

O'KANE: She told me a confidence.

KOLLVITZ: Herr O'Kane, the woman needs to answer some questions.

MALLIN: Now look Herr Kollvitz, if you've something to say, say it.

O'KANE: At last the senior officer finds his tongue.

KOLLVITZ: You occupy this privileged position in our Reich but you have not properly acquired the responsibility to go with it. You say surprisingly you never investigated her origins simply believing her lies.

MALLIN: She worked four years for an Irish banker.

KOLLVITZ: She is among other things, the sister of a Communist agitator with whom she has been in constant touch. She is knowingly a criminal activist.

MALLIN: Now wait a minute, even in these difficult times there is legality. If you wish to make accusations which we believe are untrue, you must furnish proof.

KOLLVITZ: That is coming. We have arrested the brother. It is simply a matter of time before he talks. Mr O'Kane, you agreed to our visit to the industrial complex. Yes? (*Looks at watch.*) It would be most convenient for me if we did that now. My car is downstairs.

O'KANE hesitates.

Well? Something has happened that has made you change your mind?

MALLIN: If you've made an appointment with Herr Kollvitz you'll keep it!

Pause.

O'KANE: Sure. (*To KOLLVITZ – threat.*) You and I have serious things to talk about. Lead the way.

KOLLVITZ and O'KANE exit.

After the two leave MALLIN goes and pours himself a drink of wine, sits down on the edge of his desk, looks thoughtful.

He's disturbed by the scene just witnessed. He's realising he and O'KANE are becoming vulnerable.

He drinks the wine, registers the little pile of cushions collected for a bed for CHRISTE. He lays out the cushions on the floor. He puts the greatcoat blanket over them.

To black.

Up on

Midnight. The room in darkness. Only moonlight through a window. CHRISTE is seen asleep on the cushions. Quietly O'KANE enters, tiptoes about, collects a few items from his desk drawer, puts them in a valise he's brought with him.

Then he sits down, studies the sleeping woman. Then speaks in a soft voice not to wake her and with pauses. He is not quite drunk.

The invitation to visit some industrial complex. Kollvitz, his little fart of a motor, an Opel Kadett. He's driving and silent. I make to converse. He ignores me. I ask questions. He ignores me. I ask him why he's ignoring me. He gives me a look, Christe, a cruel look, one you wouldn't see on any face except Beelzebub's – a nightmare of a look.

We reach Bergen, pass through the town, heading north. The road empties. Now it's a country lane, but the fields on each side look dead.

There's a guard house, metal gates. The guards know Kollvitz. The gates swing open. This is the camp. I have no words. I don't ask any more questions. I am too speechless. I see corpses walking. 'You'll appreciate our industrial complex,' he tells me as he drives on. It's huge. We visit the huts, crammed with – are they people? You might say, 'skin and bones', more like bones only, lying on wooden bunks, silent. 'You see,' he says, 'no bombs here. Just Jews and traitors.' We leave the camp. The little Opel makes a noise like a dentist drill. He says to me 'You are an English spy O'Kane. You owe thirty thousand Deutschmarks to your creditors in Berlin. You gather information like your colleague before you and in the diplomatic bag, it reaches someone at your Foreign Office who sells it to British Intelligence. And you hope he will pay you your share.'

'A lie,' I tell him 'a fabrication.' He says, 'When we can prove it absolutely you will see Bergen Belsen again, but not as a visitor. We are working on this proof. We'll find it.'

'You won't,' say I, 'because you're wrong.'

'I've even been to the highest authority. They are prepared for your arrest. They want proof absolute. It will be a big step for them, to arrest a diplomat however minor.' 'Minor' mind you.

Now with his spies in Dublin, he says he has spies there, would any bookie take the bet that he won't find the evidence? Of course there's a market for the bits and pieces I pick up. You see, I get into trouble. Mainly the geegees. I see horses lined up for a race, I have to bet on it. It's in the blood, the blood of Ireland. I promised you, I promised – I said I'd never abandon you. I'm sorry, real sorry. I'm a coward working for a cowards' neutral country.

God help us, I never realised that devil was after me as well as you. And… I'm terrified, terrified…

He gets up, moves quietly out.

To black.

Up on –

Morning. Day three.

MALLIN is at his desk writing his report on O'KANE. He is already suspicious that O'KANE doing a runner may somehow, however obliquely, involve CHRISTE.

CHRISTE enters from the street, sees that O'KANE is not at his desk.

CHRISTE: Mr O'Kane is late?

MALLIN says nothing, continues writing.

I will go and collect our bread. I won't be long. Herr Mallin, I haven't thanked you for letting me stay at night. I hope Mr O'Kane asked your permission.

MALLIN still says nothing. CHRISTE is puzzled.

Are you angry with me?

MALLIN: (*Sharp.*) What would I be angry about?

CHRISTE: I don't know.

MALLIN: Mr O'Kane has gone.

CHRISTE: Gone?

MALLIN: I imagine, heading back to Ireland. Did you know he was planning to leave?

CHRISTE: No.

MALLIN: Could his departure be anything to do with you?

CHRISTE: I don't understand.

MALLIN: You say you've been honest with us?

CHRISTE: Yes… I have tried to be. Why do you ask?

MALLIN: I'm expecting Herr Kollvitz.

She goes out. He resumes writing. KOLLVITZ enters.

Come in. Sit down.

KOLLVITZ: Where is Mr O'Kane?

MALLIN: I think you know that, Volker. He left a note. He says he'll take the Berlin Hanover Express, midnight. I don't think you'll catch him now.

KOLLVITZ: And Fraulein Moller?

MALLIN: Out, queuing for bread.

KOLLVITZ: Unnecessary. We have deliveries for diplomats. I am here to inform you that Fraulein Moller will no longer be working for you.

MALLIN: Really.

KOLLVITZ: It's become known that she is a Jewess. And more importantly the sister of a communist agitator arrested two days ago. Perhaps he had a weak heart. He died as we questioned him. But she may have information about his associates.

MALLIN: Jewish?

KOLLVITZ: Yes.

MALLIN: Are you saying we knew this about her?

KOLLVITZ: We are not saying that you did.

MALLIN: She told us she was German Polish. She was very convincing.

KOLLVITZ: Evidently.

MALLIN: I was writing a dispatch back to our Dublin Foreign Service about O'Kane. Do you have anything I should add?

KOLLVITZ: Does it suggest that he, like Mr Fahy, may have been gathering information about our nation to sell to British agents in your country?

MALLIN: Can you prove that?

KOLLVITZ: No.

MALLIN goes and pours a coffee.

MALLIN: I'm going to speak plainly with you, Volker.

KOLLVITZ: Careful. I am here waiting for Moller to return, not to listen to plain speaking.

MALLIN: You come from farming stock. Your dad was a farmer?

KOLLVITZ: He *is* a farmer.

MALLIN: They are hard men farmers. They make hard decisions. My father was also a farmer. Was and then wasn't. Wiped out. His history – it shows I have a bloodline of the hard stuff. Would you hear it?

KOLLVITZ shrugs.

He'd be sixty at one of the great winter storms of Sligo. Black ice, snow, winds to tear trees down. He, a dairyman, with two score cows for his living, asleep at night when the tempest struck. He would not have heard among the crashings, the gale rip his cattle shed to pieces, the only shelter for his animals. At dawn, in his fields, the cows, all quiet, all frozen, all dead. Do you know cows kneel down when they are dying – on their knees like they're praying? Sixty, and he had lost everything. Sixty, my mother forty, and mouths to feed, four children, and nothing. I had a harsh upbringing. That makes for a hard man, yes?

KOLLVITZ: So?

MALLIN: My country's enemy, and yours, the British, invented this thing. The prison camp, the concentration camp. The Boer War. Thousands died in them, women, children, and their men folk, disease, ill treatment, and starving to death. The war ended. Civilisation returned. The camps disappeared. Nightmare events of violence and cruelty are always part of great conflicts.

KOLLVITZ: What is your point?

MALLIN: All of us know, every diplomat in Berlin knows what's happening in your concentration camps. The starving, the dying, the executions.

KOLLVITZ: Of spies, Communists, Jew traitors.

MALLIN: I've heard the propaganda. But what about you Volker? What is your view? You have a view about them?

KOLLVITZ: I work to fulfil the destiny of my people. That is my view.

MALLIN: He had a way of saying it, that fuck O'Kane… Berlin station, Westermark, Rathenov, Stendal, and so on. Start down the railway line. At what station do you step off the train and shout, 'We must stop the murders in these camps!'.

KOLLVITZ: Why are you talking like this Herr Mallin?

MALLIN: I am not here to support O'Kane in any way. Our nation started with a bloody uprising. Boys of fifteen and sixteen were there with their Mausers dying, for what? For their descendants like O'Kane, corrupt, weak, not giving a shit about our land, self-centred, cynical, vile. We are young nations. Your nation started in '32, ours in 1926. Our Irish problem – corruption – buggered us from the first day. People like O'Kane's father, friend of politicians. Our Church, hating progress, wanting to keep us in a medieval doldrums. Despite some reversals I think you will win this war. And where will Ireland be then? My Ireland. I love my country. I am my country as it should be, working for it, not exploiting it. I care to be here representing it in your powerful Reich. I will not see my work destroyed by the O'Kanes, the Fahys. Do we understand each other?

KOLLVITZ: I hear you, Mr Mallin.

The door opens. CHRISTE enters with shopping basket. She takes off her coat.

MALLIN: Come in Christe.

CHRISTE: I can make fresh coffee.

MALLIN: Herr Kollvitz is not here on a social occasion. He wishes you to go with him. He says you are a Jew, illegally employed. I imagine he is right. People like him, if they know nothing, they know that.

CHRISTE: You will not allow him to do this?

MALLIN: You lied to us to obtain your position here. You lied to me, never mind the coward O'Kane. You would know the law of this city. All Jews to be registered as of two years ago. None to be employed anywhere in Berlin. You lied. You must have known if you were found out it could put difficulties in our way. It may still do so. I can't save you. I will not help you.

KOLLVITZ: Put your coat on. It is all you will need.

CHRISTE: He has no rights here. Mr O'Kane said they have no rights in this location. They need permission.

KOLLVITZ: There's no point in arguing. We found your brother and his friends. We have information concerning your contacts with them.

CHRISTE: What have you done with my brother?

KOLLVITZ: You think I'm here to answer your questions. Put your coat on.

CHRISTE goes to coat stand, takes her coat. MALLIN has gone to his desk.

CHRISTE: You are the coward, not Mr O'Kane.

MALLIN: To you maybe. To my country? I am an official of the Irish government. Nothing more, nothing less.

CHRISTE: You know what they will do to me…

MALLIN's voice rises.

MALLIN: (*To CHRISTE.*) I am not in this country in the role of judge or jury. I am not here to mouth my opinions whatever they are. I will not in any circumstance make enemies of my hosts. We, and those we employ, will obey their laws down to the last detail. That is the rule for all neutrals. I am neither here to display strength or cowardice or hatred or humanity. I am only here as the appointed legate of my nation, to represent continuously and profoundly its absolute neutrality. There is nothing else to say.

CHRISTE: So you have no voice for your own soul but can only speak the orders of others. You say your country is neutral. You're not neutral.

MALLIN: I cannot concern myself with this, with you.

CHRISTE: Yes, you offer nothing. But you did give me a time of shelter here when I could help in some way my brother's fight against these people. That time was worth everything. In the end we'll succeeed. How can men like this ever triumph? These people are an aberration. They are not part of the human race. (*To KOLLVITZ.*) I'm ready. I won't resist you. That possibility is over. And I don't wish to spend another second in this place, or in the company of this man.

KOLLVITZ tries to take her arm to steer her out, but she pushes him away and walks out. KOLLVITZ follows.

MALLIN sits at his desk, takes letter opener, opens two envelopes, reads, discards them in wastebin. He picks up pen, continues writing a report. KOLLVITZ has entered, stands by door.

Yes?

KOLLVITZ: I hope I am not disturbing you.

MALLIN: Where's the girl?

KOLLVITZ: She has been taken away by a colleague. (*Pause.*) I'm here to apologise. I should have given you advance warning about Ms Moller. That would have been the correct protocol.

MALLIN Shrugs.

You do understand that we had certain problems with your Fahy and O'Kane. But not with you, Mr Mallin. Not once with you. I would like to mention something – a real event that I read about some years ago. I must say it has defined many of my decisions, the difficult ones. May I tell you?

MALLIN: (*Flat.*) By all means.

KOLLVITZ: The story is from the days of Rome – a true story. Two centurions became the last survivors in a pitched battle with the enemy. They decided rather than to fight on hopelessly, to retreat and find and rejoin the main force of the Twelfth Legion. They were arrested in open country and brought back to Rome accused of desertion, punishable by death. Do you know this historical event?

MALLIN: No.

KOLLVITZ: Emperor Claudius visits their jail. He is a reasonable man and can save their lives. He debates with them through the night the issue whether to stand and fight to the death or more practically, rejoin the Legion and battle on. He is with them in the morning when they are crucified. He and they mutually conclude that it was their duty to stand and fight and die and not to leave the battle for whatever reason. Duty, Herr Mallin, the duty I have to my superiors. I keep that story always in front of my mind.

There is never, ever, another alternative to duty. I know I'm right, I trust you understand.

KOLLVITZ gets up, heads to the door.

MALLIN: Never doubt it, Herr Kollvitz. I too will always do my duty.

KOLLVITZ leaves.

MALLIN resumes writing, finishes off the report, starts to move slowly to front of stage reading out his report to his superiors in Dublin.

'It is a difficult time for man and conscience. Like all conflicts among nations the weak amongst us are soon revealed. O'Kane is dangerously weak in spine and intellect. That is why you must dismiss him from our Foreign Service. We are a small republic, ally of a dynamic Reich, the likely victors of this war. And they will surely need us in their victory to help them to rule defeated England. For us it will be an historic reversal of the role of subservience to the English Crown for nearly two hundred years. We must persevere meanwhile with our German comrades, and accept their excesses as the cost of moving their history, and our history, on.'

Curtain slowly begins to fall.

'As regards O'Kane's activities at gambling, I understand he had heavy financial losses, which may have tempted him to look for funds in the manner, so far suspected but unproven, of Fahy, gathering and then selling information to the enemy. I would expect nothing less of this man. He had no brains, conscience, nor decency and was without patriotism, not one single shred of it for his birthplace, his country, his Ireland…'

Curtain.

The End.